Charikleia and I dedicate this book to each other. W...
but like the cousins in the story, we live in differen...

Copyright © 2020 Elisavet Arkolaki, Charikleia ...

Translated into Italian by Tiziana Fiorito

All rights reserved.

No part of this work may be reproduced, stored in a retrieval system, or submitted in any form or by any means, electronic, mechanical, photocopying, recording or otherwise, without the prior written permission of the publisher, except in the case of brief quotations embodied in critical reviews and certain other non-commercial uses permitted by copyright law. This book may not be lent, resold, hired out or otherwise disposed of by way of trade in any form of binding or cover other than that in which it is published, without the prior written consent of the publisher. Custom editions can be created for special purposes.

For permission requests and supplementary teaching material, please write to the publisher at liza@maltamum.com www.maltamum.com

ISBN 9798710442029

My cousin and I look alike. My aunt and uncle say we look like siblings. My mommy and daddy say we look like siblings. My grandma and grandpa, the whole family, even our friends, say we look like siblings. More like twin sisters actually, like our mothers did when they were children.

Io e mia cugina ci assomigliamo. La zia e lo zio dicono che sembriamo sorelle. Mamma e papà dicono che sembriamo sorelle. Nonna e nonno, l'intera famiglia e anche i nostri amici dicono che sembriamo sorelle. Veramente sembriamo gemelle, come le nostre madri quando erano bambine.

When we were little, we lived next door to each other. To see her, all I had to do was cross the tall grass in front of our house, open the gate and enter her garden. We met every day and played all sorts of games. She was my neighbor and best friend. But then she moved.

Quando eravamo piccole, vivevamo in case vicine, l'una accanto all'altra. Tutto quello che dovevo fare per vederla era attraversare l'erba alta davanti alla casa ed entrare nel suo giardino. Ci vedevamo ogni giorno e facevamo tutti i tipi di gioco. Lei era la mia vicina e la mia migliore amica. Ma poi si è trasferita.

Now she lives in a faraway land, and I miss her so much. Mommy said to try and find something positive no matter the circumstances. There's always something to be grateful for. And so I did. My cousin and I are very lucky. Despite the distance between us, we can still talk, play, and see each other often via video chat. We talk about everything!

Ora lei vive in una terra lontana, e mi manca moltissimo. La mamma mi ha detto di provare a trovare qualcosa di positivo, a dispetto delle circostanze. C'è sempre qualcosa di cui essere grati. E così ho fatto. Io e mia cugina siamo molto fortunate. Nonostante la distanza tra di noi, possiamo ancora parlare, giocare e vederci spesso con videochat. Parliamo di tutto!

The last time we met online, she told me that it's winter and very cold there. Everything is covered in snow. She snowboards, skis, and goes ice skating with her new friends.

L'ultima volta che ci siamo viste online, mi ha detto che lì è inverno e c'è molto freddo. Tutto è ricoperto di neve. Lei fa snowboard, scia e va a pattinare sul ghiaccio con i suoi nuovi amici.

I told her that it's summer and very hot here.

Io le ho detto che qui è estate e c'è molto caldo.

I swim and snorkel every day with our old friends, and we watch the most beautiful fish underwater.

Nuoto e faccio snorkeling ogni giorno con i nostri vecchi amici, e sott'acqua guardiamo i pesci bellissimi.

Then, we spoke about animals.
She said mammals with fur white
as snow live in the
northern part of her country:
polar bears, arctic foxes, seals.

Dopo abbiamo parlato di
animali. Lei ha detto che dei
mammiferi dal pelo bianco come
la neve vivono nella regione
settentrionale del suo paese:
orsi polari, volpi artiche e foche.

I had hoped she would also talk about monkeys, but it turns out they don't live there at all!

Avevo sperato che avrebbe anche parlato delle scimmie, ma a quanto pare non vivono affatto lì!

She also asked about her pet which stayed behind with me. I answered that her cat is in very good hands and gets lots of cuddles and kisses.

Ha anche chiesto notizie del suo gatto che è rimasto qui con me. Le ho risposto che è in ottime mani e che riceve carezze e baci in abbondanza.

And I still go to the park on Sundays, and feed the ducks we both love so much.

E io vado ancora al parco la domenica e do da mangiare alle anatre che entrambe amiamo moltissimo.

Then, my cousin used some foreign words, and in an accent, I didn't recognize. I felt confused. She said she couldn't remember how to say "mountain", "rocks", and "river", and that she now talks more in her father's language.

Poi mia cugina ha usato delle parole straniere con un accento insolito che non ho riconosciuto. Mi sentivo confusa. Lei ha detto che non riusciva a ricordare come si dice "montagna", "rocce", e "fiume", e che ora usa soprattutto la lingua di suo padre.

She explained that sometimes it's hard for her to find the right words in our language. I told her I understand. I'm also learning another language at school, and it should be fun to compare words from our different languages.

Mi ha spiegato che a volte le viene difficile trovare le parole giuste nella nostra lingua. Le ho detto che capivo. Anch'io sto imparando un'altra lingua a scuola, e sarebbe divertente confrontare parole delle nostre varie lingue.

That is how we came up with the "Word Swap" painting game. My cousin painted a cactus, and then both of us said the word out loud. "Cactus" sounds the same in all our languages!

È così che abbiamo inventato il gioco di disegno "Scambio di parole". Mia cugina ha disegnato un cactus, e poi abbiamo detto insieme il suo nome ad alta voce. "Cactus" ha lo stesso suono in tutte le nostre lingue!

Her parents overheard us and joined the conversation. My aunt is a linguist and she told us that there are currently over 7,000 known spoken languages around the world! My uncle is a language teacher and he challenged us to swap a couple more words. We kept on going for a while with words like "flower", "water", "love", and "friendship".

I suoi genitori ci hanno sentite parlare e si sono uniti alla conversazione. Mia zia è una linguista e ci ha detto che attualmente ci sono più di 7.000 lingue in uso nel mondo! Mio zio è un insegnate di lingue e ci ha sfidate a scambiarci qualche altra parola. Abbiamo continuato per un po' con parole come "fiore", "acqua", "amore" e "amicizia".

Next time we video chat, I will share this painting I made for her. I would like to swap the word "home".

La prossima volta che videochattiamo, condividerò questo disegno che ho fatto per lei. Mi piacerebbe scambiare la parola "casa".

The Word Swap Game - Meet the children!

Erik, Nelly, Iason, Iria, Sadiq, Tariq, Vincent, Rukeiya, Lea, Hector, Victor, Orestis, Odysseas, Noah, Polyxeni, Lefteris, Alexis, Nikolas, Iahn, Chloe, Ioli, Rea, Nicolas, Sveva, Giuseppe, Zafiris, Dimitris, Periklis, Vaggelis, Andrea, Zaira, Philippos, Nefeli, Baby, George, Emmanuela, Mason, Ethan, Elijah, Oliver, Athina, Apolonas, Alexandros, John, Martina, Steffy, Thanos, Nikolai, Areti, Nikolai, Nina, Nicol, Joni, Mia, Emma, Stella, Artemis, Mirto, Antonis, Nicolas, Mihalis, Katerina, Nikos, Alexis, Liam, Olivia, Noah, William, Ava, Jacob, Isabella, Patricia, Hannah, Matthew, Ashley, Samantha, Maureen, Leanne, Kimberly, David, Marie, Vasilis, Yiannis, Kyra, Joakim, Alexander, Nikolas, Ellie, Sebastian, Sophie, Sabina, Stepan, Vasilis, Yiannis, Kyra, Youjin, Sejin, Okito, Magdalini, Nicoletta, Efimia, Di, Bia, Timo, Vittoria.

Dear Child,

I hope you enjoyed this story. If you'd also like to play the "Word Swap" game, ask an adult to help you, if needed, to write down your favorite word, and then draw or paint it. Your guardian can send me your painting via email at liza@maltamum.com, and I'll share it with other parents and children in my Facebook group "Elisavet Arkolaki's Behind The Book Club".

Dear Grown-up,

If you feel this book adds value to children's lives, please leave an honest review on Amazon or Goodreads. A shout-out on social media and a tag #CousinsForeverWordSwap would also be nothing short of amazing. Your review will help others discover the book, and encourage me to keep on writing. Visit eepurl.com/dvnij9 for free activities, printables and more.

Forever grateful, thank you!

All my best,
Elisavet Arkolaki

Printed in Great Britain
by Amazon